Curriculum Visions

What do we know about Jesus?

2: The Miracles

Dr Brian Knapp

Jesus telling one of his parables.

Notes

There are many translations and adaptations of the Bible. In this book we have sometimes used the King James version, but we have used many other versions and sometimes adapted them, too, depending on which seemed most appropriate for our reading level purpose and for the reading audience.

We have used capital letters to start words that refer to holy people, particularly Jesus or God (Him, He, etc). We have also used capitals when a particular event is implied, such as the Crucifixion of Jesus, but small letters when the general term is implied (e.g. crucifixion). This rule has also been applied to other holy people, such as Disciples (the 12) and disciples (general followers).

The opportunity has been taken to include works of art so that you can see the depiction of events in the eyes of some of the world's most famous historical and modern artists.

Author
Brian Knapp, BSc, PhD

Researcher
Lisa Magloff, MA

Religious Advisor
The Revd Colin Bass, BSc, MA

Senior Designer
Adele Humphries, BA, PGCE

Editor
Gillian Gatehouse

Designed and produced by
EARTHSCAPE

Printed in China by
WKT Company Ltd

What do we know about Jesus?
2: The Miracles – Curriculum Visions
A CIP record for this book is available from the British Library

Paperback ISBN 978 1 86214 564 1

Picture credits
All photographs are from the Earthscape and ShutterStock picture libraries or from public domain sources.

This product is manufactured from sustainable managed forests. For every tree cut down at least one more is planted.

Understanding others

Remember that other people's beliefs are important to them. You must always be considerate and understanding when studying about faith.

Contents

As you go through the book, look for words in **BOLD CAPITALS**. These words are defined in the glossary.

Jesus walks on water.

Jesus begins His ministry

Jesus begins by teaching to people He knew in Nazareth and at the same time He begins to gather His followers about Him.

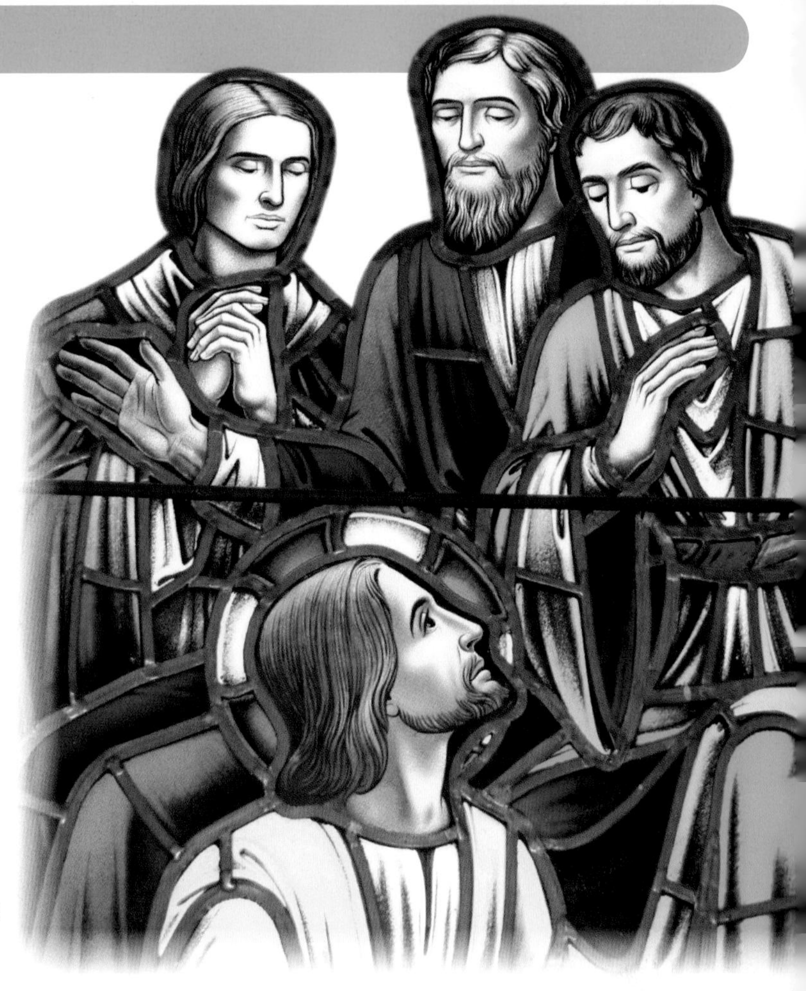

In this book you will find out about some of the amazing events that took place as soon as Jesus began His teaching (His **MINISTRY**). Of course, amazing things had happened even before Jesus was born. He was born of Mary because God decided it was time that His Son should come to Earth to help people to understand the righteous path.

Right from the start, representatives of the poor and the rich, the shepherds and the Magi, or kings, had been told where to find Jesus by God (see *What do we know about Jesus? 1: Birth & Baptism*). But the amazing power of Jesus frightened people even as He was being born. This was especially true of people who thought they had much to lose. For example, King Herod was so afraid of Jesus that he tried to make sure Jesus never lived, by ordering all first-born male babies to be killed. There would be many more people who were frightened by Jesus' power and wished Him dead, and we shall see some of these people in this book.

What Jesus had to say was unpleasant for many people. It made too much sense and threatened their comfortable ways of life. But what we shall also see is that there were many people who understood that there is more to life than wealth and power over others. They were the people who believed. Among them were the people whom Jesus chose to learn from Him – the Disciples – and all but one of them would go on to spread the word, they would become **APOSTLES**.

We begin this book after Jesus has been baptised and has gathered His Disciples. Now He feels that He has been cleansed and is ready to tell all who will hear the Good News.

Visiting the Temple

In His early years, Jesus had visited the **TEMPLE** in Jerusalem many times. It was there that people were amazed by how much He knew about religion. But as soon as Jesus began His ministry, things were different. Now the Temple and its priests were a threat, just as they felt threatened by Jesus and what He taught.

▲ A model of the Holy of Holies in Herod's Temple, Jerusalem.

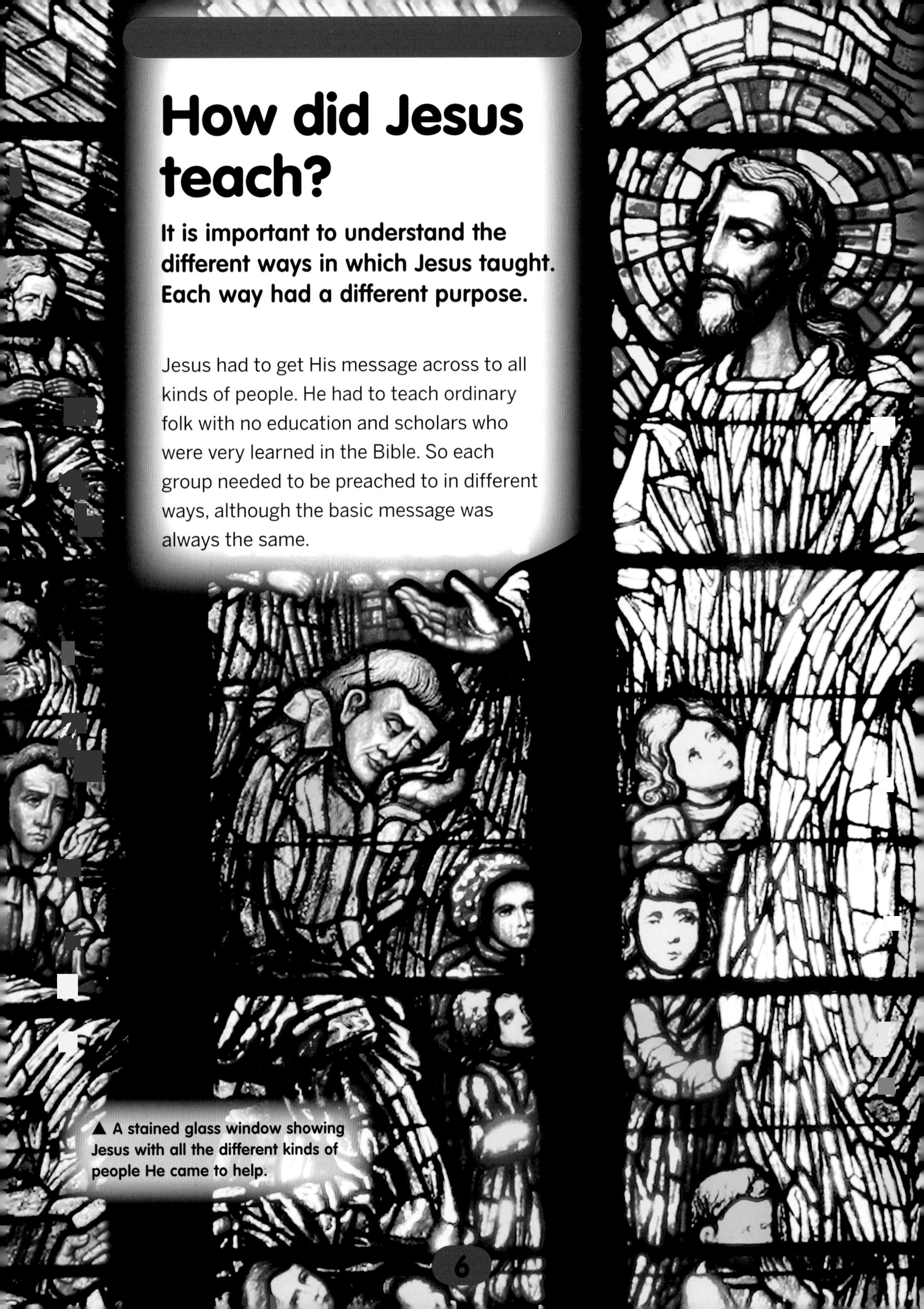

How did Jesus teach?

It is important to understand the different ways in which Jesus taught. Each way had a different purpose.

Jesus had to get His message across to all kinds of people. He had to teach ordinary folk with no education and scholars who were very learned in the Bible. So each group needed to be preached to in different ways, although the basic message was always the same.

▲ A stained glass window showing Jesus with all the different kinds of people He came to help.

Sometimes Jesus would preach in a local synagogue. But at other times, He would preach in public places where many people could gather to hear Him. But He also preached in private places, such as people's homes. This may seem odd to us, but in Jesus' time it was common for people to get together in each other's homes and listen to poets, singers, philosophers, scholars and other learned people. These kinds of teachings are called **SERMONS**.

Jesus did not only preach by giving sermons. He also taught by telling stories, called **PARABLES**. These stories are lessons in the nature of the Kingdom of Heaven, how to earn forgiveness and gain the grace of God. In a parable, an example from real life is used to stand for something else – such as an idea.

Jesus also taught by talking about real life. For example, He said, "Give to Caesar that which is Caesar's." At the time, Jews in Palestine were very upset because of the taxes they had to pay the Romans. But Jesus was telling them that there were two kinds of thing to do: to be part of the world around but, at the same time, worship God. Jesus was using the example of something that was 'in the news' to teach a lesson about God.

The other way that Jesus taught was by example, by how He lived His life and the things that He did. For example, Jesus often ate with tax collectors, prostitutes and other people who were considered 'sinners'. Jesus was also willing to preach to those that the Jews did not normally have anything to do with, such as the Samaritans. (The Samaritans lived in Samaria. They were a sect of Jews who thought their version of religion was correct and that the mainstream view was wrong. As a result, most Jews in Jesus' time ignored them.)

Jesus occasionally also showed the power of God directly. He did this through things that ordinary people could never have done. These special events are called **MIRACLES**.

We are now going to look at each of these in turn. First, the most important sermons, then some parables, and finally examples of miracles.

▲ In this stained glass window, Jesus is standing on a rock above people giving the Sermon on the Mount. The Gospel of Matthew says Jesus was seated, but the painter wanted to give Jesus extra authority by having Him standing.

The Sermon on the Mount

This is one of the most important sermons Jesus ever gave. It sets out the very basis of what Christians believe.

Although everything that Jesus said was important, and full of meaning, there were some occasions on which He said things that became the foundation of Christian belief. The Sermon on the Mount was one of these times.

Remember that Jesus was Jewish. Jewish scripture contains many laws that people are supposed to follow. The most famous of these laws are the Ten Commandments, which are a set of rules given by God to Moses on Mount Sinai. What Jesus did by giving the Sermon on the Mount was to hand His believers – those who were to become Christians – a new set of commandments. In this way He set up a new agreement between God and those who believed.

No one knows exactly where the sermon was given. It was probably given outdoors on a hill which was easy for people to reach. At this time Jesus had a great many followers and He may have chosen to give the sermon on a hill so that a large number of people could hear it. According to Matthew, Jesus gave the sermon while sitting down, with His Disciples sitting around Him and many other people making up an outer circle beyond the Disciples. This was a common way for teachers to give their talks in Jesus' time.

The sermon contains many different parts. It begins with a section called the Beatitudes, which means 'the blessings'. It talks of the types of people who will be welcomed into the Kingdom of Heaven. In Jewish worship, many sermons and actions (such as eating a meal) begin with a blessing.

The interesting thing about the Beatitudes is that it is a blessing on people who we would not normally consider blessed – the poor, the sad, the downtrodden. The meaning of the Beatitudes is that it shows that everyone is welcomed into the Kingdom of God.

Matthew 5:1–12

And seeing the multitudes, He went up into a mountain: and when He was set, His Disciples came unto Him:

And He opened His mouth, and taught them, saying,

Blessed are the poor in spirit: for theirs is the Kingdom of Heaven.

Blessed are they that mourn: for they shall be comforted.

Blessed are the meek: for they shall inherit the Earth.

Blessed are they which do hunger and thirst after righteousness: for they shall be filled.

Blessed are the merciful: for they shall obtain mercy.

Blessed are the pure in heart: for they shall see God.

Blessed are the peacemakers: for they shall be called the children of God.

Blessed are they which are persecuted for righteousness' sake: for theirs is the Kingdom of Heaven.

Blessed are ye, when men shall revile you, and persecute you and shall say all manner of evil against you falsely, for My sake.

Rejoice, and be exceeding glad: for great is your reward in Heaven: for so persecuted they the prophets which were before you.

The salt of the Earth, the light of the world

In His sermon, Jesus calls His Disciples and followers "the salt of the Earth" and the "light of the world". He is telling them that what they believe is important and that they should not hide their faith but to let it shine out so others can see it.

In ancient times, salt was a very important part of the diet. In Palestine, which was very hot in the summer, it was necessary for life. It also gave flavour to food and was used to stop food going bad. So it was central to life, just as the message Jesus was giving to His followers.

People don't hide candles, but put them high on candlesticks, so they can give light to the whole house. That is, the message should be proclaimed so that everyone in the world can hear it. That is why Jesus told His Disciples to let their light "so shine before men, that they may see your good works, and glorify your Father which is in Heaven".

Going out and telling the story of Jesus is called **EVANGELISING**, and evangelical Christians take this as the foundation for their actions. Many become **MISSIONARIES**.

▲ **Church of the Beatitudes, Galilee, is one possible location for the Sermon on the Mount.**

▶ **The Sermon on the Mount by Carl Heinrich Bloch, a Danish painter who died in 1890. The Sermon on the Mount is when Jesus made the New Covenant between mankind and God. Being seated on the Mount allowed Jesus' audience to see a parallel with Old Testament Moses being given the Ten Commandments on Mount Sinai.**

◀ A woodcut of the Sermon on the Mount.

Fulfilling the word of God

Jesus tells the gathering, the congregation, that nothing He says is intended to overturn what God has set out before. He is simply making the purpose of God's will clearer. That is why He says: "I have not come to destroy the laws of God that you already know, but to fulfil them". Jesus also reminds the congregation that they must be genuine in their beliefs. He tells them that the good works of fasting, giving to the poor and prayer are worthless when they are only done for show, and not from the heart.

Jesus then tells people not to worry about material things, such as wealth and possessions, and to seek God's Kingdom (have faith) before seeking riches on Earth.

The Lord's Prayer

The next part of the sermon contains the Lord's Prayer, which is central to all Christian belief. Jesus introduces the Lord's Prayer by saying "Pray like this." He gives the prayer as an example of what to ask from God.

Our Father, who
art in Heaven,
hallowed be Thy
name.
Thy Kingdom come,
Thy will be done,
on Earth as it is
in Heaven.
Give us this day our
daily bread.
And forgive us our
trespasses,
as we forgive
those who
trespass against
us.
And lead us not
into temptation,
but deliver us
from evil.
For Thine is the
Kingdom, the
power and the
glory, for ever
and ever.
Amen

Seeking help

Jesus told them that what He has asked would be incredibly difficult to do and that the route to **SALVATION** would be long and hard, and that many times they would stumble. But that should not put them off continuing along the path.

Jesus told them to seek help from God: "Ask, and it shall be given you; seek, and ye shall find; knock, and it shall be opened unto you."

Throwing the first stone

The teachings of Jesus were always about forgiveness, love and charity.

One of the most important of Jesus' messages was about forgiveness, which can also be thought of as love or charity.

◀ **Mary Magdalene, a sinner befriended by Jesus.**

Jesus was teaching in the Temple one day when some priests brought in a woman who had been caught having sex with a man who was not her husband. In Jesus' time, this was a crime which would be punished by stoning a person to death. The priests asked Jesus what He thought they should do with the woman. They were testing Jesus, hoping He would say something they could use against Him. But Jesus said, "He who is without sin among you, let him throw the first stone at her." Then He bent down and continued with some writing.

One by one, the priests left the room, realising that they had each committed some sin in their lives. Eventually Jesus looked up and saw that all the priests had left and only the woman was still there and He said, "Woman, where are your accusers? Did no one condemn you?" She said, "No one, Lord." Jesus said, "Neither do I condemn you. Go your way." But Jesus then added these vital words: "From now on, sin no more."

Jesus not only forgave the woman for her sins, but He pointed out that everyone has sinned, and so everyone is in need of forgiveness, and that everyone should try harder to do what is right.

Washing of feet

Another time, Jesus was eating dinner in the home of a priest named Simon. A prostitute, who was one of Jesus' followers, came and sat at Jesus' feet weeping. She washed His feet with her tears and wiped them with her hair. Then she kissed Jesus' feet and rubbed them with ointment.

The priest was astonished because he felt that if Jesus knew what kind of woman she was, He would never have let her touch Him. So Jesus said, "Simon, I have something to tell you. A certain lender had two debtors. The one owed five hundred denarii, and the other fifty. When they couldn't pay, he forgave them both. Which of them therefore will love him most?"

Simon answered, "The one whom he forgave the most."

Jesus said, "You have judged correctly." Turning to the woman, He said to Simon, "Do you see this woman? I entered into your house, and you gave Me no water for My feet, but she has wet My feet with her tears, and wiped them with the hair of her head. You gave Me no kiss, but she, since the time I came in, has not ceased to kiss My feet. You didn't anoint My head with oil, but she has anointed My feet with ointment. Therefore I tell you, her sins, which are many, are forgiven, for she loved much. But to whom little is forgiven, they will love back with little."

Turn the other cheek

Jesus also urged people not to seek vengeance, but to give people a chance to repent. Jesus explained that vengeance is when they ask for an eye for an eye, and a tooth for a tooth. However, that is not the way. Instead, if someone strikes you on the right cheek, turn the left cheek to him rather than seek vengeance.

In Christianity, forgiveness is also bound up in the notion of love and charity. In the Christian sense, charity is a type of love – love of one's fellow human beings. To forgive is to show charity and love, and this brings one closer to God.

When Jesus was asked by a lawyer, what he should do in order to enter the Kingdom of Heaven. Jesus asks the lawyer what is written in Jewish law, and the lawyer answers, "You shall love the Lord your God with all your heart, with all your soul, with all your strength, and with all your mind; and your neighbour as yourself." Jesus tells him that this is correct, that the way to Heaven is by loving your neighbour.

◀ This painting by Bout shows the anointing of Jesus by Mary in Simon's house, as the other guests look on astonished.

The parables

To show people how they can enter the Kingdom of Heaven and be saved, Jesus used simple stories with deeper meanings. We call them parables.

It may be that Jesus used parables because He wanted people to go away and think about the meanings, for that was a common teaching method used by the ancient Greeks.

The weeds

The Kingdom of Heaven can be imagined as being like a farmer who sowed good seed in his field. But while he slept, his enemy came and sowed weeds among the wheat, and then crept away. As the wheat grew, the weeds also grew.

The farmworkers came and asked him why weeds were growing where they thought he had planted only good seed. He told them that an enemy had done it. So the workers asked if they should go into the fields and clear out the weeds. But the farmer told them to let everything grow, then take up the weeds and burn them, and only after that gather up the wheat and take it to his barn.

In this parable, the person who sows the good seed is Jesus, the field is the world; the good seeds are people who follow Jesus' teachings; and the weeds are evil people. The enemy who sowed the weeds is the Devil. The harvest is the end of time, and the reapers are angels. Eventually, evil people will go to hell and all the good people will be taken to God.

This is where you will find all of the parables in the New Testament

1. **Drawing in the net** *Matthew 13:47–50*
2. **Workers in the vineyard** *Matthew 20:1–16*
3. **Lost money** *Luke 15:8–10*
4. **The faithful servant** *Luke 12:35–48*
5. **The good Samaritan** *Luke 10:30–37*
6. **The seed growing secretly** *Mark 4:26–29*
7. **The lost sheep** *Matthew 18:12–14, Luke 15:1–7*
8. **The mustard seed** *Matthew 13:31–32, Mark 4:30–32, Luke 13:18–19*
9. **The pearl** *Matthew 13:45–46*
10. **The prodigal son** *Luke 15:11–32*
11. **The sower (the four soils)** *Matthew 13:3–23, Mark 4:1–20, Luke 8:5–15*
12. **The wedding feast** *Matthew 22:1–14, Luke 14:16–24*
13. **Pharisee and the publican** *Luke 18:9–14*
14. **Ten talents** *Matthew 25:14–30, Luke 19:11–27*
15. **The budding fig tree** *Matt 24:32–36, Mark 13:28–32, Luke 21:29–33*
16. **The friend at night** *Luke 11:5–8*
17. **The hidden treasure** *Matthew 13:44*
18. **The importunate widow** *Luke 18:1–8*
19. **The leaven** *Matthew 13:33, Luke 13:20–21*
20. **The master and servant** *Luke 17:7–10*
21. **The rich fool** *Luke 12:16–21*
22. **The rich man and the beggar** *Luke 16:19–31*
23. **The tares or weeds** *Matthew 13:24–30*
24. **The ten virgins** *Matthew 25:1–13*
25. **The two debtors** *Luke 7:41–47*
26. **The two sons** *Matthew 21:28–32*
27. **The unjust steward** *Luke 16:1–9*
28. **The wicked husbandmen** *Matthew 21:33–46, Mark 12:1–12, Luke 20:9–19*
29. **The wise and the foolish builders** *Matthew 7:24–27*
30. **Unmerciful servant** *Matthew 18:23–35*
31. **Building a tower and waging war** *Luke 14:28–33*
32. **The barren fig tree** *Luke 13:6–9*
33. **The guests,** *Luke 14:7–15*

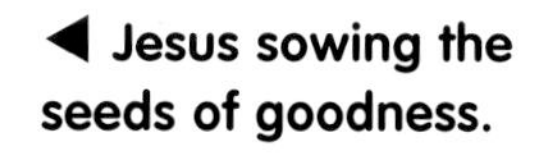

◀ Jesus sowing the seeds of goodness.

Workers in the vineyard

The Kingdom of Heaven can be thought of as being like a farmer who went out to hire labourers to work in his vineyard. The farmer agreed with some workers to pay them a penny a day. After three hours it was clear that more people were needed, so the farmer went into the market and found other people idle. He told them to go to the fields and he would give them their just reward. He did the same after six and eleven hours.

At the end of the day, the farmer told his manager to pay the workers starting with those who had worked for the shortest time. But he had agreed with everyone that he would pay them a penny. At this the people who had worked for longest grumbled. But the farmer replied that he had not cheated them because he had paid what he agreed.

Just as the labourers who were hired last got paid the same as the labourers who had worked all day, people who hear Jesus' message late in life will be saved just as much as people who hear it early in life. The important thing is your belief, not how long you believe for.

The rich man and the beggar

There was a rich man who lived in luxury. A beggar named Lazarus lived at his gate. Lazarus was covered with sores and longing to eat what fell from the rich man's table. The time came when the beggar died and the angels carried him to Abraham's side in Heaven. The rich man also died and was buried. In Hell, where he was in torment, he looked up and saw Abraham far away, with Lazarus by his side. So he called to him, "Father Abraham, have pity on me and send Lazarus to dip the tip of his finger in water and cool my tongue, because I am in agony in this fire." But Abraham replied, "Son, remember that in your lifetime you received your good things, while Lazarus received bad things, but now he is comforted here and you are in agony. And besides all this, between us and you there is a great chasm." He answered, "Then I beg you, father, send Lazarus to my father's house, for I have five brothers. Let him warn them, so that they will not also come to this place of torment." Abraham replied, "They have Moses and the Prophets; let them listen to them." "No, Father Abraham," he said, "but if someone from the dead goes to them, they will repent." He said to him, "If they do not listen to Moses and the Prophets, they will not be convinced even if someone rises from the dead."

This parable reminds people not just to look after themselves, but also after others who are less fortunate. It also explains why Jesus did not return to Earth after the short period of the **RESURRECTION**, that is everyone now had all the information they needed. The rest is faith.

▼ **The parable of the rich man and the beggar from the Codex Aureus of Echternach.**

Lazarus at the rich man's door.

Lazarus' soul is carried to Paradise by two angels (left), and Lazarus at Abraham's side (right).

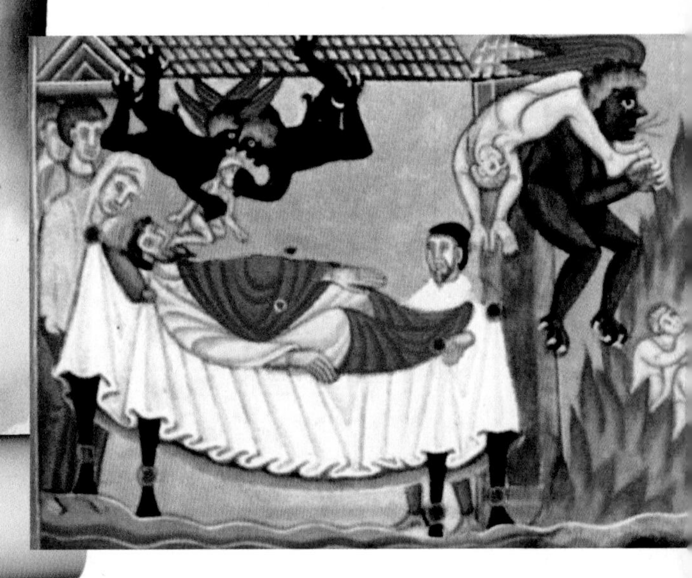

The faithful servant

Jesus told a parable about the strength of your faith. Always be ready, like those who are waiting for their master to return from the wedding banquet, so that they may open the door for him as soon as he comes and knocks.

Blessed are those servants whom the master finds alert when he returns. If he returns during the middle of the night, or near dawn, and finds them awake, then they shall also be blessed. But if that servant says to himself, "My master is delayed in coming", and if he begins to beat the other servants and to eat and drink and get drunk, the master of that servant will return on a day when he does not expect him and at an hour that he does not know, and will cut him in pieces, and put him with the unfaithful. That servant who knew what his master wanted, but did not prepare himself or do what was wanted, will receive a severe beating. You also must be ready, for the Son of Man is coming at an unexpected hour.

Peter said, "Lord, are you telling this parable for us or for everyone?" And the Lord said, "Blessed is that servant whom his master will find at work when he arrives. Truly I tell you, he will put that one in charge of all his possessions. From everyone to whom much has been given, much will be required; and from one to whom much has been entrusted, even more will be demanded."

Here Jesus is saying that you simply never know when the Day of Judgement will be, and so you must remain faithful to God all of the time. But, more than this, if, by the Day of Judgement, you have been especially fortunate in life, you will be expected to return that gift in being more responsible for those who have been less fortunate.

The rich man's soul is carried off by two devils to Hell and tortured.

The lost sheep

When the Pharisees again complained about how Jesus was spending all His time with sinners, Jesus told another story, that of the lost sheep. In this story, Jesus asked, "Which of you, if you had one hundred sheep, and lost one of them, wouldn't you leave the other ninety-nine in the wilderness, and go after the one that was lost, until you found it? When you have found it, you would carry it on your shoulders, rejoicing. When you come home, you would call together your friends and his neighbours, saying to them, 'Rejoice with me, for I have found my sheep which was lost!'"

Jesus then said: "I tell you that there will be more joy in Heaven over one sinner who repents, than over ninety-nine righteous people who need no repentance."

▼ **The Good Samaritan by Rembrandt.**

The good Samaritan

On one occasion an expert in the law stood up to test Jesus. "Teacher," he asked, "what must I do to inherit eternal life?" "What is written in the Law?" He replied. "How do you read it?" He answered: "Love the Lord your God with all your heart and with all your soul and with all your strength and with all your mind"; and, "Love your neighbour as yourself." "You have answered correctly," Jesus replied. "Do this and you will live." But he wanted to justify himself, so he asked Jesus, "And who is my neighbour?" In reply Jesus said:

"A man was going down from Jerusalem to Jericho, when he fell into the hands of robbers. They stripped him of his clothes, beat him and went away, leaving him half dead. A priest happened to be going down the same road, and when he saw the man, he passed by on the other side. When another priest came to the place and saw him, he, too, passed by on the other side. But then a Samaritan (someone of a different Jewish sect) came where the man was; and when he saw him, he took pity on him. He went to him and bandaged his wounds, pouring on oil and wine. Then he put the man on his own donkey, took him to an inn and took care of him. The next day he took out two silver coins and gave them to the innkeeper. 'Look after him,' he said, 'and when I return, I will reimburse you for any extra expense you may have.'"

Jesus then asked: "Which of these three do you think was a neighbour to the man who fell into the hands of robbers?" The expert in the law replied, "The one who had mercy on him." Jesus told him, "Go and do likewise."

This parable is told by Jesus in order to show that you must not just follow the exact words of the Biblical law, but also fulfil the spirit of the law.

Ten talents

This parable tells of a master who was leaving his home to travel, and before going gave his three servants different amounts of money. On returning from his travels, the master asked his servants to tell him what they had done with the money given to them. The first servant reported that he was given five talents (coins), and he had made five talents more. The master praised the servant as being good and faithful, gave him more responsibility because of his faithfulness, and invited the servant to be joyful together with him.

The second servant said that he had received two talents, and he had made two talents more. The master praised this servant in the same way as being good and faithful, giving him more responsibility and inviting the servant to be joyful together with him.

The last servant who had received one talent reported that knowing his master was a hard man, he buried his talent in the ground for safekeeping, and therefore returned the original amount to his master. The master called him a wicked and lazy servant, saying that he should have placed the money in the bank to generate interest or to have used in some other beneficial way.

The master commanded that the one talent be taken away from that servant, and given to the servant with ten talents, because everyone that has much will be given more, and whoever that has a little, even the little that he has will be taken away. And the master ordered the servant to be thrown outside into the darkness where there is "weeping and gnashing of teeth."

This is a hard parable to understand. Is it telling us that we should try to make more and more money? Hardly. It is telling us that we should try to make the best of ourselves, whatever gifts we have been given, for that is what the Lord will judge us on at the Day of Judgement. So we should not sit around and be idle (bury our talent in the ground), but make as much of our abilities as we can for the sake of everyone, not just ourselves.

▲ The parable of the ten talents from an 18th century woodcut.

Talent
A talent was a vast amount of money (about 20 years' wages for a labourer). Five talents would have paid 100 labourers for a year. So 5 talents could have been used to set up a business, make a profit and also pay many other people a year's wages. That is, there is a lot of good that could be done with it.

The prodigal son

This story was told after the Pharisees complained that Jesus was eating with sinners.

The story is about a man who has two sons. The younger son asks his father to give him his portion of the family estate as an early inheritance. Once he received it, the son promptly set off on a long journey to a distant land and began to waste his fortune on wild living. When the money ran out, a severe famine hit the country and the son found himself in real trouble. He took a job feeding pigs, but he ended up so poor and hungry that he even thought about eating the food given to the pigs.

The young man finally came to his senses, and remembered his father. He decided to return to his father and ask for forgiveness and mercy.

The father, who had been watching and waiting, received his son back with open arms. He was overjoyed by the return of his lost son and gets his servants to prepare a feast in celebration.

All of the time the younger son had been away, the older son had been working in the fields and helping his father make ends meet. On the evening that the younger son returned, he came back from the fields and discovered a feast in progress. The older son was not at all happy, but his father explained

▼ **The return of the prodigal son by Gustave Doré.**

that the older brother's jealousy was wrong by saying, "You are always with me, and everything I have is yours, but it was right to celebrate and be glad, for this, your brother, was dead, and is alive again. He was lost, and is found."

In this parable, Jesus is telling His followers of the Father's love, showing that He will welcome us home, however foolish we have been, provided we are sorry.

▼ Rembrandt, Return of the prodigal son.

The hidden treasure

This is one of the shortest of the parables. It is just one sentence:

The Kingdom of Heaven is like treasure hidden in a field, which a man found and covered up; then in his joy he goes and sells all that he has and buys that field.

This parable tells us that some rewards are great enough to be worth great sacrifices: the man may have to sell all that he had in order to be able to buy the field, but when he buys the field, he gains the treasure in it, which is worth more than all that he sold. Jesus told this parable to express the idea that even if living according to God's commandments was a difficult thing to do and demanded great sacrifices, they would result in the reward of the Kingdom of Heaven.

▼ **Rembrandt, The parable of the hidden treasure.**

▼ The wise and foolish virgins, 1813, by Peter von Cornelius.

The ten virgins

This story is told by Jesus at a party of girls given the honour of attending a wedding. Each of the ten girls is carrying a lamp as they await the coming of the bridegroom. Five were wise and brought a jar of oil to top up the lamp. The other five were foolish and took no oil with them. The bridegroom was unexpectedly delayed and the girls' lamps began to burn low. The foolish girls asked the wise ones for some of their spare oil, but the others refused, saying that they might then not have enough for themselves and everyone would have suffered. So the foolish girls had to go and buy some more from a nearby shop.

While the foolish girls were away buying more oil, the bridegroom arrived. The wise girls were there to welcome him and the foolish ones arrived too late and were locked out.

This is one of three parables in *Matthew, Chapter 25* that form a unit about entering the Kingdom of Heaven. Seen together the messages are: be prepared, do your best and love your neighbour. In this, the first of the three, the important message is 'keep awake', that is be prepared.

Why did Jesus perform miracles?

Jesus is famous for performing many miraculous things, every one of them with a wider meaning and purpose.

Jesus did many things: He tried to teach peace and understanding; and He tried to explain better the meaning of the Bible. Yet any good **RABBI** could have done that. What Jesus did, was to show people that He was not as other people, but really was the **MESSIAH** they had been waiting for.

Why should He do this? Because people are not easy to convince, especially in matters as important as faith.

Jesus is connected to many miracles (including those connected with His birth and death). The miracles are not evenly spaced through Jesus' ministry. Many of them come early on, when He was gathering His followers. It was also a fantastic and powerful way of getting His story spread by word of mouth. After all, who would not rush to tell others when they had just witnessed a miracle?

Some people might argue that miracles were just magic tricks. But Jesus did not perform miracles just to amuse the crowd. He did it out of compassion for people. So by performing miracles of healing, Jesus is showing people the importance of charity and love, and the power of His teachings.

Annunciation *Luke 1:26–38*
Miraculous baptism *Matthew 3:13–17, Mark 1:9–11, Luke 3:21–22, John 1:32–34*
Angels protect Jesus in the desert *Matthew 4:11, Mark 1:12–13*
Conversion of Nathanael *John 1:45–51*
Water into wine *John 2:1–11*
Exorcism in Capernaum *Mark 1:21–28, Luke 4:31–37*
Healing *Matt 4:23–25, Mark 1:39*
Fishers of men *Luke 5:1–11*
Exorcises demons *Matt 7:22, Mark 9:38–40, 16:17, Luke 9:49–50, 10:17, John 1:12–13. 2:23, 3:18, 14:13–14, 17:11–12, Acts 3:6, 4:10, 4:30, 16:18, 19:11–20*
Cured a leper *Matt 8:1–4 Mark 1:40–45, Luke 5:12–16*
Samaritan woman *John 4:28–29*
Centurion's boy-servant *Matt 8:5–13 Luke 7:1–10*
Royal official's son *John 4:46–54*
Peter's mother-in-law's fever *Matt 8:14–17, Mark 1:29–34, Luke 4:38–41*

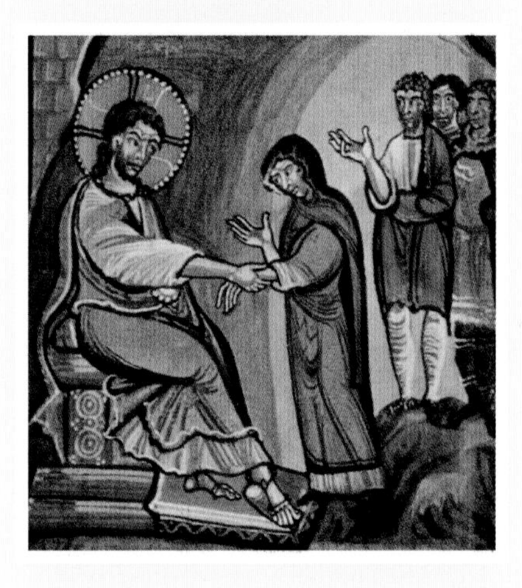

◄ Jesus healing Peter's mother-in-law, 11th century.

Drove demons out of Mary Magdalene *Mark 16:9, Luke 8:2*
Calmed a storm *Matt 8:23–27, Mark 4:35–41, Luke 8:22–25*
Demons and pigs *Matt 8:28–34, Mark 5:1–20, Luke 8:26–39*
A paralytic at Capernaum *Matt 9:1–8, Mark 2:1–12, Luke 5:17–26*
A paralytic at Bethesda *John 5:1–18*
Raised the son of a widow at Nain *Luke 7:11–17*
Raised Jairus' daughter *Matt 9:18–26, Mark 5:21–43, Luke 8:40–56*
Healed a woman who touched Jesus *Matt 9:20–22, Mark 5:24–34, Luke 8:43–48*
Healed two blind men *Matt 9:27–35*
Twelve Apostles given their authority *Matt 10:1, 10:8, Mark 3:13–15, 6:7, Luke 9:1*
Miracles at Chorazin, Bethsaida, Capernaum *Matt 11:20–24, Luke 10:13–15*
Healed a man's withered hand *Matt 12:9–13, Mark 3:1–6, Luke 6:6–11*

▲▼ *(above)* The mountain on which Jesus performed the Miracle of the Transfiguration. In this miracle, Jesus is transfigured, He becomes radiant, speaks with Moses and Elijah, and is called "Son" by God. *(below)* Mount Tabor in Israel, traditionally identified as the place on which the Transfiguration miracle occurred.

Healed huge crowds *Matt 12:15–21, Mark 3:7–12, Luke 6:17–19*
A house divided *Matt 12:22–32, Mark 3:20–30, Luke 11:14–23; 12:10*
The loaves and fishes *Matt 14:13–21, Mark 6:30–44, Luke 9:10–17, John 6:1–14*
Walked on water *Matt 14:22–33, Mark 6:45–52, John 6:15–21*
Curing those who touched His garment *Matt 14:34–36, Mark 6:53–56*
Cured a Canaanite woman *Matt 15:21–28, Mark 7:24–30*
Healed a deaf-mute *Mark 7:31–37*
Healed large numbers *Matt 15:29–31*
Fed four thousand *Matt 15:32–39, Mark 8:1–10*
Restored a man's sight at Bethsaida *Mark 8:22–26*
Transfiguration of Jesus *Matt 17:1–13, Mark 9:2–13, Luke 9:28–36, 2 Peter 1:17–18*
Cured a possessed boy *Matt 17:14–21, Mark 9:14–29, Luke 9:37–43*
Paid tax with a coin from a fish's mouth *Matt 17:23–27*
Healed a woman on the Sabbath *Luke 13:10–17*
Cures even though King Herod wanted to kill him *Luke 13:31–32*
Raised Lazarus *John 11:1–44*
Healed a man with dropsy *Luke 14:1–6*
Healed ten lepers *Luke 17:11–19*
Healed large crowds in Judea *Matt 19:1–2*
Healed two blind men *Matt 20:29–34*
Healed Bartimaeus *Mark 10:46–52, Luke 18:35–43*
Blind man given sight *John 9*
Healed blind and lame at Herod's Temple *Matt 21:14*
Cursed a fig tree *Matt 21:18–22, Mark 11:12–14, 11:20–25*
Transubstantiation of bread and wine at the Last Supper *Matt 26:26–30, Mark 14:22–26, Luke 22:14–20, John 6:48–66, 1 Cor 11:23–26*
Makes Judas betray Him *John 13:26–30*
Healed soldier's ear *Luke 22:49–51*
Crucifixion eclipse *Matt 27:45, Mark 15:33, Luke 23:44–45*
Earthquake when Jesus died *Matt 27:50–54*
Empty tomb *Matt 27:62–28:15, Mark 16:1–8, Luke 24:1–12, John 20:1–10*
Resurrection appearances *Matt 28:9–10, 28:16–20, Mark 16:9–18, Luke 24:13–49, John 20:11–23, Acts 1:1–8, 2:24, Romans 10:9, 1, Cor 9:1, 15:1–15*
Ascended to Heaven *Mark 16:19–20, Luke 24:50–53, John 20:17, Acts 1:9–11*
Doubting Thomas *John 20:24–31*
Catching of fish after Resurrection *John 21:1–14*
Miraculous conversion of Paul *Acts 9:1–19,22:1–22,26:9–24*
Descended into Hell *Ephesians 4:8–10, Acts 2:27, 2:31, 1, Peter 3:19–20, 4:6,*
Holy Spirit *Matt 3:10–12, Mark 1:8, Luke 3:16–17, John 14:16, 14:26, 15:26, 16:7, Acts 1:5, 1:8, 2:4, 2:38, 11:16*
Rich young man raised from the dead *Secret Gospel of Mark 1*

This is why so many miracles are about healing the sick. But at the same time He was, of course, completely aware of the effect miracles would have on those around – and on those who ruled. Jesus performed miracles in order to show that He was sent by God.

Miracles and the Biblical prophecies

One important thing to remember about the miracles is that many of them were designed to match prophecies from the Old Testament (Jewish Bible). The prophecies would all have been known to the Jews of first century Palestine. For example, they would have known about all of the prophecies relating to the coming of the Messiah.

Faith

The people who wrote the **GOSPELS** wanted to appeal to a wide audience. To do this, they wanted to make sure that Jesus' message would appeal to both Jews and non-Jews. So they included stories showing that all people can be saved through faith and belief in Jesus' message.

Healing the sick

Most of the miracles in the Gospels are about healing the sick, the lame, the deaf and the blind. In the Jewish community at that time the law laid down that people were impure if they were not physically and mentally well. So anyone who was ill was thought of as impure. These people could not make a sacrifice in the Temple, and if they could not do that they could not enter the Kingdom of God.

So, in healing the sick and making people with mental problems well, Jesus was sending a powerful signal — that these people were just as entitled as anyone else to enter the Kingdom of God. The fact that the cures are done by Jesus Himself carried a further layer of meaning — that Jesus had the authority to decide who could or could not enter the Kingdom of God.

Jesus performed several miracles where He 'rid people of demons', whether that be healing mentally ill people or symbolically freeing people from sin or bad behaviour.

▶ **Jesus healed many sick and mentally ill children.**

Nicodemus

Early in Jesus' ministry, a rabbi named Nicodemus saw Jesus performing a miracle and said that no one could perform such miracles unless they were sent by God. Jesus said, "Most certainly, I tell you, unless one is born anew, he can't see the Kingdom of God."

Nicodemus wondered what Jesus meant – how could a person be born a second time? Jesus explained that, in order to enter the Kingdom of Heaven, a person has to be reborn in spirit.

Nicodemus was still a bit confused about what this meant, so Jesus went on to explain that God had sent Him not to judge people but to save people. Whoever believes in Jesus as the Messiah will be saved.

Jesus was saying that He had come to bring salvation (light), and that those who are evil will not believe in Him and so will not be saved, but that those who do believe will be saved. Jesus was speaking about Jews when He said this, but the message applies to anyone – anyone who believes in Jesus' message can be saved.

Now read about some of the more famous miracles:

Water into wine

Jesus performed His first miracle – turning water into wine – in the village of Canaan, in Galilee. He chose this because it has a deep symbolic meaning, which would have been clear to the Jews of first century Judea.

On the third day after His baptism, Jesus was attending a wedding in Canaan. Jesus' mother, Mary, was also there. At this time, wine was served as part of the wedding feast, and to run out of wine would have been seen as an insult to the guests – as a lack of hospitality.

But, unfortunately, the wine did run out very early in the feast – a major embarrassment to the bride and groom. So Jesus' mother said to Him that there was no more wine. "Why do you involve Me?" Jesus replied. "My time has not yet come."

Nevertheless, His mother told the servants to do whatever Jesus asked of them. Jesus told the servants to fill some large water jars to the brim. Then He told them to take some of the water to the wedding table. When the water was tasted, it was found to be a very fine wine.

In fact, the wine was so good that one of the important guests commented on how generous the groom was to continue to serve such good wine when people usually served the poorer wine late in the feast.

As a result of the miracle, the Disciples believed in Him.

Jesus didn't tell anyone what He had done, although Jesus' mother, the servants and the Disciples knew. Turning water into wine may seem a bit of a party trick, but this miracle had great symbolic value. For example, in the Jewish prophecies, there would be a future time when there would be enough food and drink for everyone. The prophecies also tell that this will be the time when the Messiah comes down to Earth. Jesus was reminding His Disciples of the prophecy of plenty, and He was telling them that He was sent by God to fulfil this prophecy. To the Disciples, it meant they were not just in the presence of a great prophet, but of the Messiah Himself.

The nobleman's son

Shortly after changing the water into wine, Jesus was in Galilee. A nobleman came up to Him and begged Him to come and heal his son, who was close to death. Jesus said to him, "Unless you see signs and wonders, you will in no way believe." The nobleman said to Him, "Sir, come down before my child dies." Jesus said to him, "Go your way. Your son lives."

The nobleman believed Jesus and as he was returning home, his servants came up to him and told him that his son was indeed alive. The man asked them when he began to recover and his servants told him that it happened the day before at the seventh hour – the exact hour when the nobleman was talking to Jesus. The nobleman and all of his household now believed in Jesus' powers.

This story gives us one reason why Jesus performed some of his miracles. Jesus says, "Unless you see signs and wonders, you will in no way believe." In other words, people will not believe He is the Messiah unless He performs miracles.

We might ask, why then doesn't Jesus perform some more spectacular miracles that can be seen by more people? But remember that in first century Judea (and everywhere else for that matter), medicine was very primitive. People suffered from many illnesses that we cure easily today. To perform a showy miracle might have impressed people, but it would not have helped them. By healing illnesses, Jesus is showing people that He loves them and has come to show them love.

A man with leprosy

A leper came to Jesus and kneeling down in front of Him, begged Jesus to heal him, saying "If you want to, you can make me clean."

Jesus was moved with compassion, He stretched out His hand, and touched the leper (not something that anyone else would have done), and said to him, "I want to be made clean." Jesus then told the leper to go to the priest. The reason for that was Jewish law had very strict requirements to prove that a leper had been cured and they could only be agreed to by a priest. But the law made it virtually impossible for anyone to be proved cured. In fact, the Jewish people thought that only the Messiah would be able to heal leprosy. So, in this way, Jesus was telling the priest that He was the Messiah.

Of course, the leper went and told everyone how he was cured and as a result huge crowds began to gather around Jesus everywhere He went.

The paralysed man

As the news of Jesus' remarkable healings spread, more and more people came to hear Him and brought their sick and dying loved ones to Him. Although Jesus regularly withdrew to be alone and pray, He spent much of the time besieged by desperate people, hanging on His every word.

One day, Jesus was in the small town of Capernaum. He was teaching inside a house, and the house was packed with people. Some of the crowd were locals, but Luke says there were also Pharisees and officials. These officials had travelled from every village in Galilee, and from Judea and Jerusalem, to hear Him. They sat and listened, but they had their own reasons for attending: they were afraid because He was a threat to their authority. There were plenty of rumours about Him, and now they had come to see for themselves.

While He was teaching, some men came to the house, carrying a paralysed man on a mat. They tried to take him into the house to lay him before Jesus. When they could not find a way to do this because of the crowd, they went up on the roof and lowered him on his mat into the middle of the crowd, right in front of Jesus.

Jesus realised their desperate actions showed their faith in Him. He told the man that his sins had been forgiven. He then told the man to get up and go home. On finding he could, the man got up and went home praising God.

In the Jewish faith, only God can forgive sins. Of course, for Jesus' followers, it showed them that Jesus was the Messiah. But there were two groups who were not convinced: the rabbis and priests. It simply reinforced what they already believed.

The healing of a mentally ill man

On the shores of the Sea of Galilee is a town which in Jesus' time was known as Gerasa. It was not a Jewish town; in fact devout Jews weren't supposed to go there. This is because people who were mentally ill or '**POSSESSED**' lived here, among the tombs and caves on the outskirts of the town.

Jesus and His Disciples arrived at the town by sea. As soon as they got out of their boat, a man who had been living in the tombs in the town came up to Him. He constantly cried out and cut himself with stones. People tried to tie him down, but he always broke free.

When this man saw Jesus approach, he ran and bowed down to Him, and cried out "What have I to do with You, Jesus, You Son of the Most High God?" Jesus understood that this was the voice of the 'demon' and He sent the demon away from the man.

The people from the town came to see what had happened. They saw the possessed man sitting in his right mind, and they were afraid. They began to beg Jesus to leave their town. As He was getting into the boat, the man who had been possessed asked to come with Jesus. But Jesus said to him, "Go to your house, to your friends, and tell them what great things the Lord has done for you, and how He had mercy on you."

The boy with epilepsy

In this story, Jesus' Disciples tried but could not heal a boy who had had epilepsy since he was a child. Jesus told His Disciples that this was because they didn't have enough faith.

When the boy was brought before Jesus, he began to writhe about and foam at the mouth. Then Jesus spoke and the boy instantly became still, almost as though he were dead. But Jesus took him by the hand and he got up. It was another miracle.

The faith of a Greek woman

In another story, Jesus casts demons out of the daughter of a Greek woman. This story is important because it shows that Jesus was willing to help anyone with faith, not only Jews.

Jesus was staying with his Disciples and a woman came to the house and begged Him to cast the 'demon' out of her daughter. Jesus told her that He was here to save the Jewish people and to heal Jewish people.

But the woman replied, "Yes, Lord. Yet even the dogs under the table eat the children's crumbs."

Jesus was moved by the woman's humbleness and faith and told her that the demon had now left her daughter.

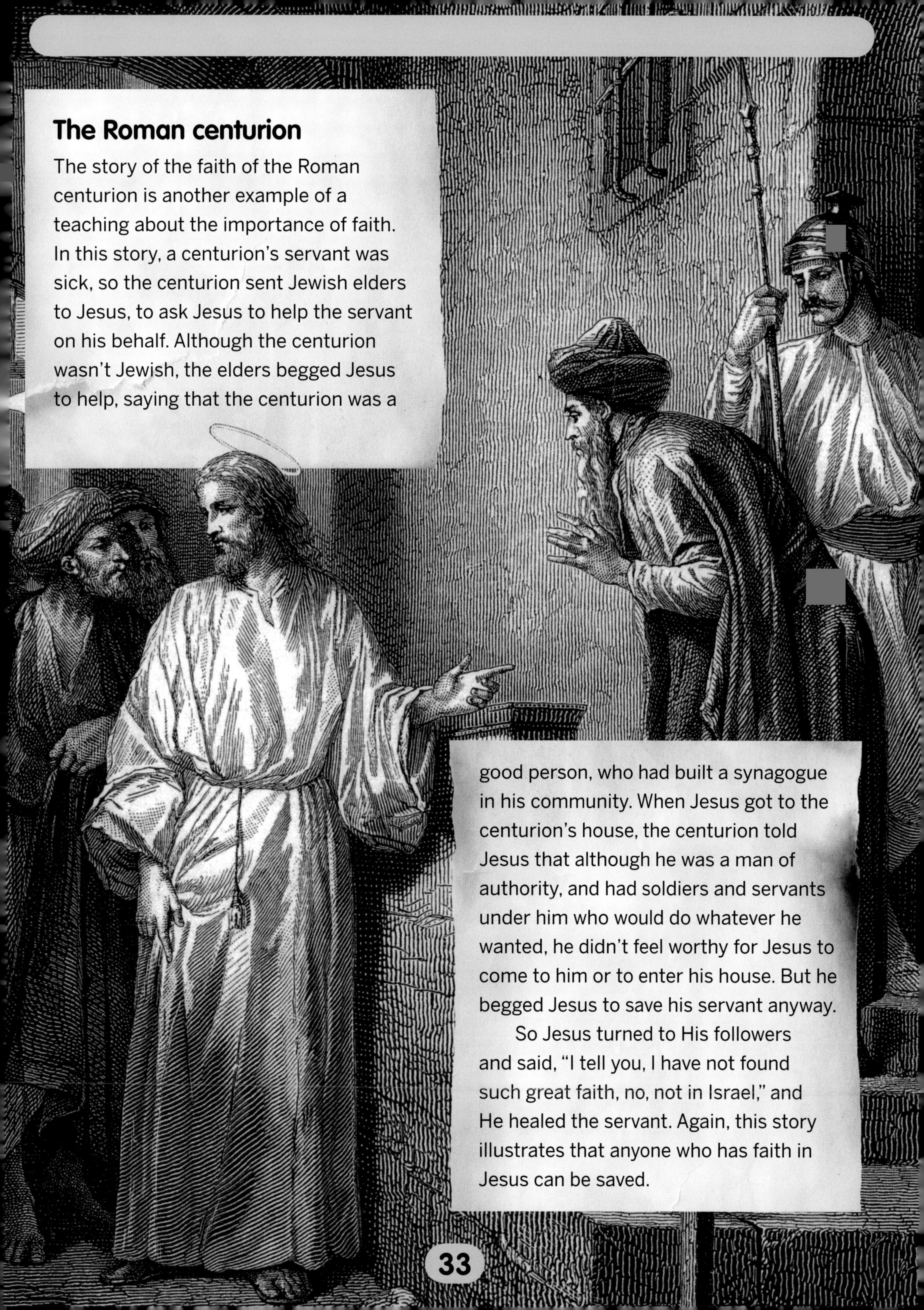

The Roman centurion

The story of the faith of the Roman centurion is another example of a teaching about the importance of faith. In this story, a centurion's servant was sick, so the centurion sent Jewish elders to Jesus, to ask Jesus to help the servant on his behalf. Although the centurion wasn't Jewish, the elders begged Jesus to help, saying that the centurion was a good person, who had built a synagogue in his community. When Jesus got to the centurion's house, the centurion told Jesus that although he was a man of authority, and had soldiers and servants under him who would do whatever he wanted, he didn't feel worthy for Jesus to come to him or to enter his house. But he begged Jesus to save his servant anyway.

So Jesus turned to His followers and said, "I tell you, I have not found such great faith, no, not in Israel," and He healed the servant. Again, this story illustrates that anyone who has faith in Jesus can be saved.

The miracle of stilling the storm

One day, as Jesus and the Disciples set out on one of their many trips across the Sea of Galilee, they were hit by an unexpected and violent storm. The Disciples struggled to keep the boat under control in the storm, but the boat was nearly swamped. Remember that many of the Disciples were fishermen, so this must have been a very bad storm if they could not control the boat.

Sudden violent storms from the east are common in the Sea of Galilee in the early evenings of winter.

While the Disciples were fighting for their lives to control the boat, Jesus was sleeping. The Disciples woke Him and told Him that they thought they were about to drown. So Jesus got up and told the wind and the waves to be calm. Then Jesus said to His Disciples, "Why are you so afraid? Do you still have no faith?" The Disciples would have made the connection with a passage from *Psalm 107* (see opposite) immediately as they watched Jesus command the storm. Jesus was showing that He had control over everything, Jesus was acting as if He were God.

Today, this story is often told to help Christian people who are upset to feel more calm, by saying that belief and faith in God can calm storms – not only on the sea, but in our lives as well. But the Disciples knew that if the rabbis and priests found out about this miracle, they would certainly arrange for Jesus to be killed as a **BLASPHEMER**.

▼ A stained glass window showing Jesus walking on water. Note: all of the miracles on this spread are nature miracles rather than healing miracles.

Psalm 107:23–30

They that go down to the sea in ships, that do business in great waters;

These see the works of the Lord, and His wonders in the deep.

For He commandeth, and raiseth the stormy wind, which lifteth up the waves thereof.

They mount up to the Heaven, they go down again to the depths: their soul is melted because of trouble.

They reel to and fro, and stagger like a drunken man, and are at their wit's end.

Then they cry unto the Lord in their trouble, and He bringeth them out of their distresses.

He maketh the storm a calm, so that the waves thereof are still.

Then are they glad because they be quiet; so He bringeth them unto their desired haven.

Walking on water

This miracle happened immediately after the miracle about the feeding of the 5,000 (the loaves and fishes miracle, see pages 38–39). Jesus told the Disciples to return to the fishing village of Bethsaida and leave Him to go to the mountain to pray on His own. Later that night, the Disciples were crossing the Sea of Galilee in a fishing boat and making little progress against the strong wind. Suddenly they saw Jesus walking on the water. At first they thought it must be a ghost, but Jesus reassured them, telling them, "Take heart, it is I! Do not be afraid!" Then Jesus got into the boat.

As usual, the miracle has deeper meanings. In the years after the Crucifixion of Jesus, the newly formed Christian church faced opposition from the Jews and persecution by the Romans. To many of these early Christians, the Church must have felt like the fishing boat on the Sea of Galilee, buffeted by strong winds and rocked by the waves. But the message of the miracle is that they should not be afraid: Jesus had not abandoned them, He was with them. It is just that His time frame and theirs might not be the same, because they could only see the present, whereas Jesus could see forever.

Catching lots of fish

Jesus performed the miracle of catching a huge number of fish twice. These miracles are meaningful not so much for what they are as for when they happen.

The first time was shortly after Jesus was baptised by John the Baptist. Jesus was standing by the water's edge and was surrounded by a crowd of people who wanted to hear Him preach. He saw two boats standing by the lake, but the fishermen were not in them because they were washing their nets. Jesus climbed in to one of the boats, which happened to belong to Simon Peter, and asked him to push out a little way from the land. Jesus then sat down and preached from the boat. When He had finished speaking, Jesus told Simon Peter to sail into deeper waters and let his nets down.

Simon Peter could not see the point of this because they had already tried catching fish and there were none there. However, he did as he was asked. When he lowered the nets there were suddenly so many fish in the net, that it was near to breaking with the weight of fish and he had to get help from the other boat.

▲ **Jesus helping the fishermen to catch lots of fish. Look carefully at Jesus to see if this is the first time this miracle was performed or the last time (after Jesus' Resurrection).**

Simon Peter fell down at Jesus' knees because he realised that Jesus had come from God and felt he was unworthy.

But Jesus told Simon Peter, "Come after Me, and I shall make you fishers of men"

It was after this miracle that the four fishermen left their boats and nets and followed Jesus.

Following this miracle, Jesus had four Disciples – all fishermen. Jesus performed a miracle He knew they would understand – that of making a huge number of fish come into their nets.

Fish after Resurrection

Much later in the New Testament, Jesus performs a similar miracle for the same people. This time it is after He has been crucified and been resurrected. His Disciples are aimless and frightened, their Lord has been killed and they are unsure what to do. They did not know that Jesus had been resurrected.

At the sea of Tiberias, several Disciples decided to go fishing (remember these men were all fishermen before they met Jesus), but all night they caught nothing. In the morning they saw a man standing on the beach who asked them if they had anything to eat. But of course they had caught nothing. So He told them to cast their net on the right side of the boat. Suddenly it was so full of fish that they couldn't even lift it into the boat. Then they recognised that it was Jesus. When they all got to shore, Jesus asked them to bring some of the fish that they had just caught, and together they ate breakfast.

In this story, we see a mirror of the first one, when the Disciples recognise Jesus because of the miracle of catching lots of fish. Jesus is showing His Disciples that He is always with them – as it was when they first met, so it will be to the end.

The miracle of the loaves and fishes

(Also called the feeding of the 5,000.) One day, Jesus had been teaching the Disciples, but they were always surrounded by people wanting to listen to Jesus and asking Him to heal them. So Jesus and the Disciples went far from the nearest town to get some peace and quiet. But the people followed them out to the desert. When Jesus saw the huge crowd, He had compassion on them and began teaching them.

When evening came, the Disciples suggested that Jesus should send the crowd away so they could walk into town and buy some food. But Jesus told the Disciples that there was no need for the people to leave, and that the Disciples should feed them. Of course, the Disciples told Jesus that they didn't have enough money to buy all the food needed for thousands of people.

So Jesus asked the Disciples, how many loaves they had, to which the answer was five – and two fish. Jesus told them to sit all the people down in groups of hundreds and fifties. Taking the five loaves and the two fish and looking up to Heaven, Jesus gave thanks and began to break the bread and divide the fish and hand them to the crowd. As He prayed, the bread kept breaking and the fish kept dividing until everyone was fed.

After everyone was full, the Disciples picked up twelve basketfuls of leftover pieces of bread and fish.

This story is more than just miraculously making bread and fish appear from thin air

– it is about Jesus' role as the Messiah and Saviour of the Jewish people. This miracle was a reminder of the prophet Moses.

Many centuries before, Moses had freed the Hebrews from slavery in Egypt and had led them on the treacherous journey to freedom. This is one of the most important events in Jewish history.

After Moses and the Hebrews had fled from Egypt and crossed the Red Sea, they found themselves in the barren Sinai desert. The Hebrews asked Moses how on earth they were going to find enough to eat in the desert. Moses ordered the Hebrew people to sit down and be patient. Thereafter, in the mornings, the people found that the ground was covered with food – manna (the bread of Heaven) – like a fall of snow. In the evenings, the skies above the camp were alive with small edible birds.

So now you can see why Jesus chose those numbers and those groups. In the miracle of the loaves and fishes, Jesus divides His followers into groups of 100 and 50, and has His Disciples hand out the loaves and fishes, which He had miraculously made appear. To Jesus' followers, all of this would have reminded them instantly of the events connected to Moses.

The story could also have reminded Jesus' followers of King David, the Jewish King who built the Temple. When David first ran from King Saul, he fed his small group of followers with the priest's bread, asking the priest, "Give me 5 loaves, or whatever you have". So Jesus was choosing to compare Himself with a new King David. The 12 baskets of food were meant to remind people that there had been enough food for everyone, as the Jews often spoke of Israel as the '12 tribes'. Of course, the number 12 of the Apostles that followed Jesus was also meant to represent the leaders of the New 12 tribes of Israel.

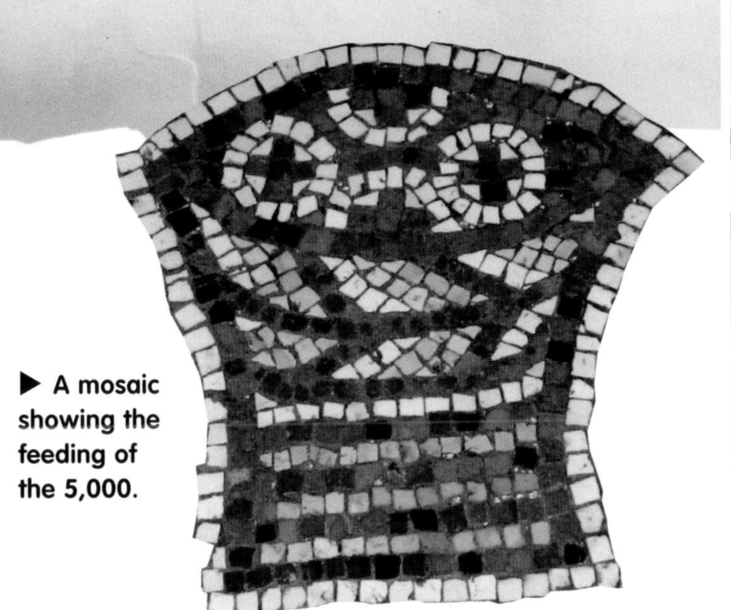

▶ **A mosaic showing the feeding of the 5,000.**

▲ **The Church of the Multiplication was built over the place where some people think the loaves and fishes miracle happened.**

Jesus brought people back from the dead three times. They were signs that Jesus was more than a prophet, that He was the Son of God. Here are two of the stories. The third one is about the daughter of the religious leader Jairus.

Raising the widow's son

In this story, Jesus went to a town called Nain, and His Disciples and a large crowd went along with Him. As He approached the town gate, a dead person was being carried out – the only son of a widow. A large crowd from the town was attending the funeral. When Jesus saw the woman, His heart went out to her and He said, "Don't cry."

Then He went up and touched the coffin, and those carrying it stood still. He said, "Young man, I say to you, get up!" The dead man sat up and began to talk.

All the people watching were filled with awe and praised God. "A great prophet has appeared among us," they said. "God has come to help His people."

As usual, this miracle is a reminder of a miracle from the Jewish Bible that took place a thousand years earlier and was performed by one of the holiest men in Jewish history – the prophet Elijah.

The story – as told in the book of *Kings (1 Kings 17:18–24)* – tells how Elijah was staying with a widow in a small town when her son fell ill. The woman – though poor – had been welcoming to Elijah, so he was distressed to see the son die, so he asked God to bring him back to life. Elijah gave him back to his mother and said, "Look, your son is alive!" So the miracle of raising from the dead was meant to remind people of Elijah.

Raising Lazarus

The raising of Lazarus is one of Jesus' best known miracles. According to John, this is the miracle that seals Jesus' fate as far as the high priests are concerned. This is actually a very long story, and it begins with Lazarus falling ill.

Lazarus was the brother of Mary and Martha. Lazarus fell sick and Mary and Martha sent for Jesus. Instead of leaving right away, Jesus stayed where He was for two days, saying, "This sickness is not death, but for the glory of God, that God's Son may be glorified by it."

When Jesus arrived in Bethany, Judea, He found that Lazarus had already been dead and in his tomb for four days and the town was full of mourners.

▲ Resurrection of Lazarus, painted by Juan de Flandes, around 1500.

Martha met Jesus on the road and told Him off for arriving too late to save her brother. When Jesus told Martha her brother would rise again, Martha thought He was talking about the Resurrection on Judgement Day, but Jesus said, "I am the Resurrection and the Life. He who believes in Me will still live, even if he dies. Whoever lives and believes in Me will never die. Do you believe this?" She said to him, "Yes, Lord. I have come to believe that You are the Christ, God's Son, He who comes into the world."

Later, Jesus saw Mary and she also told Him off for arriving too late. Then they went to the tomb and Jesus said, "Take away the stone." They took away the stone, Jesus lifted up His eyes, and said, "Father, I thank You that You listened to Me. I know that You always listen to Me, but because of the multitude that stands around I said this, that they may believe that You sent Me." When He had said this, He cried with a loud voice, "Lazarus, come out!"

▼▶ A 16th century painting *(below)* of Raising Lazarus (by Juan de Flandes) compared to a modern Orthodox painting *(right)* of the same scene.

At this, Lazarus came out of the tomb and the people began to believe in Jesus as the Messiah.

This was the last straw as far as the chief priests were concerned. Jesus was now openly saying that He was the Son of God. The priests were very worried about the effect this might have on the people and how the Roman rulers might behave. They might see it as a rebellion and massacre everyone. They decided that, instead, Jesus must die.

People doubt Jesus

There were several occasions on which the people He was preaching to did not believe Jesus, or became very angry with Him.

When Jesus began preaching, He was not popular with everyone. The priests and leaders, for example, objected to what Jesus said because it was against what they thought of as Jewish laws and customs. Other people did not believe that Jesus was the son of God and so they felt He was being **BLASPHEMOUS** by saying He was.

The people in Jesus' home area around Nazareth were the first who rejected Him. This was because they knew His family and had grown up with Jesus, and so they felt it was not possible that He could be the Son of God.

▲ Jesus declares that the scripture is fulfilled.

One Sabbath, Jesus went to the synagogue to read a section of the Jewish Bible during worship (a different section is read out each week). It was the part of the *Book of Isaiah* where it was written:

"The Spirit of the Lord is on me, because He has anointed me to preach good news to the poor. He has sent me to heal the brokenhearted, to proclaim release to the captives, recovering of sight to the blind, to deliver those who are crushed, and to proclaim the acceptable year of the Lord."

After Jesus read these lines, He closed the book, gave it back to the attendant, and sat down. Everyone in the synagogue was wondering what Jesus was going to say. Everyone's eyes were on Him.

Then, quite remarkably, Jesus told the people in the synagogue that He was the Messiah – He said, "Today, this scripture has been fulfilled in your hearing."

At first the town's people were impressed that Jesus had read so beautifully. Then they began to think about what Jesus had really meant, that is He had effectively dared to call Himself the Messiah. Jesus told them that no prophet is welcome in His hometown. Jesus then said that in the Jewish Bible (Old Testament) the prophets only help those who believe, so that even the people of Nazareth would suffer if they did not listen to Him and repent.

Jesus pointed out that in the days of the prophets, when Elijah was healing people, the person he healed of leprosy was a Syrian woman, and a non-Jew at that. With this, Jesus seems to be saying that He had been sent by God to tell them that everyone was welcome in the Kingdom of God.

When the people of Nazareth heard all this, they got very angry and threw Jesus out of the synagogue and out of the village. A crowd even tried to push Jesus to the top of a hill and throw Him off the cliff. But Jesus calmly walked through the crowd and went on His way.

▼ Jesus is almost driven from the cliff edge by the people of Nazareth.

Even Jesus' followers sometimes found it hard to believe Him. This is why, after Jesus had been preaching for a while, His Disciples asked Him for a sign. They asked Him to send manna (bread) from Heaven – like Moses did in the Jewish Bible. But Jesus told them instead that the very life of the world was the bread of God and went on to say, "I am the bread of life. He who comes to Me will not be hungry, and he who believes in Me will never be thirsty... This is the will of the One who sent Me, that everyone who sees the Son, and believes in Him, shall have eternal life; and I will raise him up at the last day."

Jesus angers the priests

As Jesus continued to preach, and as His teachings became more and more popular, the priests kept trying to show that He was committing blasphemy.

It is easy to get confused between the rituals that priests have thought up and the laws given by God. In Jesus' time the priests distrusted Jesus because He preached things that weakened their power and that were against Jewish belief at the time.

As a result, the priests and rabbis grew more and more upset with Him, and eventually decided that He was dangerous and needed to be killed (see *What do we know about Jesus? 3: The Crucifixion*).

One day, for example, some priests saw Jesus' followers eating a meal without washing first. One Jewish law is that people should wash and say a blessing before eating. They were not concerned about hygiene and the passing on of germs because they didn't know about such things at the time. Rather, they were concerned about following a ritual for its own sake.

The priests told Jesus off for allowing His followers to disobey this traditional law. But Jesus called the priests hypocrites, saying that they forced people to follow many laws and traditions which did not come from God, but were made up by people.

Calling His followers, Jesus said that food in itself cannot be unclean, or sinful, only our actions and thoughts can be unclean. Food passes in and out of the body and becomes waste, and this is just the natural order of life, so it can't be sinful. But sins such as evil thoughts come out of the body so they are the things that make you unclean, because they are things that we have control over.

When the Disciples pointed out that what Jesus said had offended the priests, He said that the priests would not be saved, since they didn't believe in Jesus' teachings, so don't worry about them.

On another day, Jesus' followers went out to pick grain on the Sabbath, so they could make bread to eat. The priests asked Jesus why His followers were working on the Sabbath. Jesus responded by telling a story from the Old Testament, of how the prophet David once took the bread from the Temple, which only the priests were allowed to eat, and gave it to his followers because they were hungry. Jesus then said,

"The Sabbath was made for man, not man for the Sabbath. Therefore the Son of Man is Lord even of the Sabbath."

In the Gospel of Mark, there is a story of how the priests and rabbis even became angry with Jesus for healing the sick on the Sabbath. One of the Jewish commandments is for people to do no work on the Sabbath.

Jesus said: "Is it lawful to do good on the Sabbath days by healing, or to do evil, by doing nothing? That is to save life, or to kill?"

They had no answer to this.

Throughout all of these stories is the theme that Jesus is able to reinterpret the commandments because He is the Messiah and the Son of God.

God is making a new agreement with people, through Jesus, one in which the old laws need to be seen in a fresh light. This is the agreement that Christians have taken up.

▼ **Jesus and His Disciples picking the corn on the Sabbath and angering the priests.**

Jesus talks about His death

Jesus often talked about His death even many years before it happened. Here are some of the things He said.

Jesus' ministry lasted for three years. Throughout His ministry, and especially towards the end, Jesus gave hints to His followers that He would not be with them for long. For example, in *John 7:1–13*, Jesus' family is encouraging Him to come to Jerusalem to celebrate the feast of the Tabernacles (Sukkot), a Jewish holy day. But Jesus tells them He can't because He has many enemies in Jerusalem and, "My time has not yet come. The world can't hate you, but it hates Me, because I testify about it, that its works are evil. You go up to the feast. I am not yet going up to this feast, because My time is not yet fulfilled."

Jesus is saying that if He went, He would be killed, but it is not yet His time to be killed. His choice of words "not yet" tells us that He knows the time for His death will be coming soon.

As it happened, Jesus went to Jerusalem quietly to heal the sick anyway in a public bath just outside the city walls, although He was spotted after performing some miracles on the Sabbath, something that further enraged the priests.

Jesus predicts His end

On another occasion, after the miracle of the feeding of the five thousand, Jesus told His Disciple Peter that He would give him

the keys to the Kingdom of Heaven and that he would be the foundation of the Christian Church (see Bible quotation above). Jesus then told His Disciples that He must soon go to Jerusalem, how He would suffer, how He would be killed and that He would rise again on the third day.

▲ **This mosaic shows the occasion when Jesus told the Disciples they have the keys to the Kingdom of Heaven.**

When Peter tried to tell Him that this need not come to pass, Jesus said the famous words: "Get thee behind Me, Satan."

What He was saying was that He could not be tempted to spare Himself from what God had planned. That would be the easy way, and the way of the Devil (Satan).

Then Jesus said to His Disciples "If any man will come after Me, let him deny himself, and take up his cross, and follow Me. For whosoever will save his life shall lose it: and whosoever will lose his life for My sake shall find it. For what is a man profited, if he shall gain the whole world, and lose his own soul? Or what shall a man give in exchange for his soul?"

Here, Jesus is telling His followers that life in this world is unimportant, that if they believe in God, they can be unafraid of death, because they will live again with God. Jesus' words, "let him take up his cross and follow Me" also tells how He will meet His end.

As Jesus gets closer to the time when He will be killed, His predictions about His own death become more detailed. Shortly after He arrived in Jerusalem for the last time, Jesus told His followers not to be afraid of death.

Jesus also gives the reason why He has to die. By dying, even though He knows exactly how it will happen and so could easily avoid it, Jesus is demonstrating that there is nothing to be afraid of in death – those who believe in Him will live forever, so there is no point in fearing death.

Jesus goes on to tell His followers that He will be resurrected after death so they can all see for themselves that there is nothing to fear in death. In other words, Jesus is dying so that He can be resurrected and prove that belief can save you from eternal death.

The next stage

Each time Jesus hints or tells His followers that He will be killed before too long, they protest and become upset, but each time Jesus tells them that they shouldn't worry – He will be reborn with God. This is the real meaning of Jesus' message, that belief will save the believer and allow them to be reborn and live with God forever.

How this all came about we shall see in the third book of this series, which details the Passion and the Resurrection.

Glossary

Apostles People 'sent out'. The Twelve of Jesus' inner circle of Disciples whose task was to found the Christian Church and spread the Good News.

Blasphemer/Blasphemous The disrespectful use of the name of God.

Evangelise To spread the Good News about Jesus, the Resurrection, the Holy Spirit and Salvation for the faithful.

Gospel The 'Good News'. The first four books of the New Testament: the Gospel of Matthew, Gospel of Mark, Gospel of Luke and Gospel of John.

Messiah Jewish word for the saviour of Israel. The Greek word is Christ.

Ministry The teaching of beliefs.

Miracle Something that could not be explained by the laws of nature and which causes wonder and understanding of God's ways.

Missionary A religious person who tries to convert those of a different, or no, faith.

Parable A short story that illustrates a religious lesson.

Possessed A mentally ill or disturbed person. Ancient peoples thought they were 'possessed' by devils.

Rabbi A Jewish religious teacher. Also used to mean someone superior to yourself.

Resurrection The coming back to life of Jesus after His death.

Salvation Everlasting life with God.

Sermon A religious teaching from a pulpit or some other place where people are gathered for worship.

The Temple The main temple of the Jewish nation in Jerusalem. It had been founded by Kind David and built by King Solomon and rebuilt by King Herod.

Index